"*A Girl's Story* is a profound and beautiful examination of the impenetrable wall that time erects between the self we are, and the selves we once were. I know of no other book that so vividly illustrates the frustrations and the temptations of that barrier, and our heartache and longing in trying to breach it. Annie Ernaux is one of my favorite contemporary writers, original and true. Always after reading one of her books, I walk around in her world for months."
—SHEILA HETI, author of *Motherhood* and *How Should a Person Be?*

"Ernaux, one of France's leading contemporary writers, mines her shame to good effect. There's no hysteria or prurience in her writing; she approaches her history with precision, never sentimentality. . . . Revisiting painful periods is hardly new territory for writers, but Ernaux distills a particular power from the exercise. As she puts it, 'I am endowed by shame's vast memory, more detailed and implacable than any other, a gift unique to shame.'"
—JOUMANA KHATIB, *The New York Times Book Review*

"Written in 2013, although coming out a few years later, *A Girl's Story* predates Me Too as a narrative genre, but Ernaux's body of work speaks to the simplest and possibly best thing Me Too offered women. It is her foundational exigency: how to remember politically, in collective form. . . . Across the ample particularities of over 40 years and 21 books, almost all short, subject-driven memoirs, Ernaux has fundamentally destabilized and reinvented the genre in French literature."
—AUDREY WOLLEN, *The Nation*

"Annie Ernaux writes memoir with such generosity and vulnerable power that I find it difficult to separate my own memories from hers long after I've finished reading. In *A Girl's Story* she detangles an adolescence rife with desire and shame, an era of both internal and external debasement. Ernaux wisely ventures into the gray areas of her memories; she doesn't attempt to transcend their power, nor to even 'understand' them, but to press them firmly into this diamond of a book."
—CATHERINE LACEY, author of *Pew and The Answers*

"Ernaux . . . writes with clear, controlled precision that is as vivid as it is devastating to read, and which connects the pain and indignity of her experience to class, power and patriarchy."
—*The Guardian*

"*Happening* is gripping and painfully inevitable to read—like a thriller. I felt close to Annie Duchesne, in her aloneness, in a way I've rarely felt close to a character in a book. Women will be grateful to Ernaux for her wisdom, concision, and commitment to writing about death and life."
—DAISY HILDYARD, author of *The Second Body*

"Ernaux's work is important. Not just because of her subject matter, but because of the way she hands it over: the subtle contradictions; her dispassionate stoicism, mixed with savagery; her detailed telling, mixed with spare, fragmented text . . . These are not things we vote for. These are not things we judge. These are things that happen. Are happening."
—*Irish Times*

"*The Years* is an earnest, fearless book, a *Remembrance of Things Past* for our age of media domination and consumerism, for our period of absolute commodity fetishism."
—EDMUND WHITE, *The New York Times Book Review*

"In this devastating yet deceptively simple work of autofiction, Annie Ernaux retraces the origins of her identity as an artist to the height of the Algerian War, and the loss of her innocence at the cusp of womanhood. Sifting through the wreckage of her memory, she queries its nature: whether we possess it, construct it, or view it like a photograph, or as a form of cinema; whether, long suppressed, it may be resurrected and reconstituted as narrative—and where, in such an act, the author ends and the character of the author begins. 'What is the belief that drives her, if not that memory is a form of knowledge?' she asks. In *A Girl's Story*, Ernaux cements her position as a writer of immense depth and grace."
—SARAH GERARD, author of *Sunshine State*

"Annie Ernaux is ruthless. I mean that as a compliment. Perhaps no other memoirist—if, in fact, memoir-writing is what Ernaux is up to, which both is and isn't the case—is so willing to interrogate not only the details of her life but also the slippery question of identity. . . . Think of *The Years* . . . as memoir in the shape of intervention: 'all the things she has buried as shameful and which are now worthy of retrieval, unfolding, in the light of intelligence.'"
—DAVID L. ULIN, *Los Angeles Times*

"The process of reading *The Years* is similar to a treasure box discovery. . . . It is the kind of book you close after reading a few pages, carried away by the bittersweet taste it leaves in your mind. . . . Ernaux transforms her life into history and her memories into the collective memory of a generation."
—AZARIN SADEGH, *Los Angeles Review of Books*

THE YOUNG MAN
ANNIE ERNAUX

Translated by Alison L. Strayer

SEVEN STORIES PRESS
New York · Oakland

Originally published in French as *Le jeunne homme* (Paris: Gallimard, 2022).

Photos courtesy of the author.

Seven Stories Press
140 Watts Street
New York, NY 10013
www.sevenstories.com

Library of Congress Cataloging-in-Publication Data is on file.

College professors and high school and middle school teachers may order free examination copies of Seven Stories Press titles. Visit https://www.sevenstories.com/pg/resources-academics or email academic@sevenstories.com.

Printed in the United States of America

9 8 7 6 5 4 3 2 1

If I don't write things down, they haven't been carried through to completion, they have only been lived.

CONTENTS

THE YOUNG MAN

Five years ago, I spent an awkward night with a student who had been writing to me for a year and wanted to meet me.

Often I have made love to force myself to write. I hoped to find in the fatigue, the dereliction that comes after, reasons not to expect anything more from life. I hoped that orgasm, the most violent end to waiting that can be, would make me feel certain that there is no greater pleasure than writing a book. Perhaps it was the desire to spark the writing of a book—a task I had hesitated to undertake because of its immensity—that prompted me to take A. home for a drink after dinner at a restaurant, during which, through timidity, he had remained all but speechless. He was almost thirty years younger than me.

We saw each other on weekends, and, in between, came to miss each other more and more. He phoned me daily from a public phone so as not to arouse the suspicions of the girl he lived with. Neither she nor he, caught up in the routines of a couple living together too young, and worrying about exams, had ever imagined that making love could be anything other than a more or less slow-motion satisfaction of desire; that it could be a sort of continuous creation.

The fervor he displayed in the face of this new discovery bound me to him more and more. Little by little, the affair became a relationship that we longed to take to the limit, without really knowing what that meant.

When, to my satisfaction and relief, he broke up with his girlfriend and she left the apartment, I got into the habit of staying at his place from Friday night to Monday morning. He lived in Rouen, the city where I too had lived as a student, in the sixties, but for years had only driven through to visit my parents' graves in Y. As soon as I arrived, abandoning in the kitchen, not yet unpacked, the bags of provisions I had brought, we made love. There would already be a CD in the player, usually the Doors, which started to play as soon as we entered the bedroom. At some point, I ceased to hear the music.

The powerful chords of "Love Street" and the voice of Jim Morrison entered my consciousness again. We remained lying on the mattress, on the floor. Traffic was heavy at that hour. The beams of headlights flickered on the walls of the room through the high bare windows. I felt as if I had been lying on a bed since age eighteen and never risen from it—the same bed but in different places, with different men, indistinguishable from one another.

His apartment looked out on the Hôtel-Dieu, decommissioned the year before and under construction, soon to become the main prefecture. In the evening, the windows of the building were illuminated and often remained that way throughout the night. The big square courtyard in front was an expanse of pale empty shadow behind the closed iron gates. I looked at the black roofs, the dome of a church looming in the background. Apart from the security guards, there was no longer anyone there. It was to that place, that hospital, where I had been transported, as a student, one January night, because of a hemorrhage resulting from a backstreet abortion. I no longer knew in which wing the room I had occupied for six days was located. There was, in this astonishing, almost uncanny coincidence, a sign of a mysterious encounter and a love story that had to be lived to the fullest.

On Sunday afternoons when it was drizzling outside, we stayed in bed, and eventually dropped off, or faded in and out of sleep. From the silent street came the voices of rare passersby, usually foreigners from a nearby hostel. Then, I felt as if I were back in Y., where, as a child, I would read beside my mother, who had fallen asleep from exhaustion on her bed, fully dressed, after Sunday lunch, when the shop was closed. I became ageless and drifted between one time and another in a semiconscious state.

At A.'s place, I was transported back to the discomfort and the makeshift amenities I too had known when my husband and I were starting out as students. On the electric hot plate, whose thermostat no longer worked, all that could be cooked were steaks, always in danger of sticking to the pan the moment you put them in, or pots of pasta and rice which overflowed in uncontrollable floods of boiling water. The old fridge, whose temperature could not be adjusted, froze the lettuce in the salad drawer. You had to wear three sweaters to withstand the damp cold of the high-ceilinged rooms with their poorly sealed windows, impossible to heat even with the electric heaters that were ruinously expensive to operate.

He took me to Le Bureau and Big Ben, cafés frequented by young people. He treated me to meals at Jumbo. His favorite radio station was Europe 2. Every evening he watched *Nulle part ailleurs.** The people he greeted on the street were always young, often other students. When he stopped to talk, I stood aside; they watched me sidelong. Afterwards, he would relate the academic background of the guy he had just talked to, with all the details of his successes and failures. Sometimes, discreetly, from a distance, asking me not to turn around, he would point out a prof from the department of literature where he studied. He

---

* A French entertainment cult hit on Canal+, 1987 to 2001; a combination of talk show, news, music, satire (including *Les nuls* and *Les guignols de l'info*).

tore me away from my generation, but I was not part of his.

His extreme jealousy—he accused me of having had a man around to my house because the toilet seat was raised—made it pointless to doubt his passion for me and rendered absurd the reproach I suspected his friends of leveling at him, "How can you go out with a menopausal woman?"

He was devoted to me with a fervor which, at fifty-four, I had never experienced with any other lover.

Forced to contend with the instability and destitution to which poor students are exposed (his parents had debts and lived on the outskirts of Paris on a secretary's salary and the wages from a government-assisted employment contract), he bought only the cheapest products or the ones that were on sale—Laughing Cow cheese in prewrapped portions, five-franc wheels of Camembert. He went all the way to the Monoprix to buy his baguette because it cost fifty centimes less than the ones at the nearby bakery. His gestures and reflexes were dictated by a continual, inherited lack of money. He possessed a kind of resourcefulness that helped him get by on a daily basis. When at a big supermarket, seize a handful of cheese samples from the plate held out by the food demonstrator; in Paris, to relieve yourself without paying, enter a café with a purposeful manner, locate and use the toilets, and come out looking casual; check a parking ticket machine to see what time it is (he didn't have a watch), etc. He played the soccer Lotto every week, staking everything, as it is natural to do when in a constant state of need, on luck. "I'll win one day, it's inevitable." Sundays in the late morning he watched *Téléfoot* with Thierry Roland. The moment when the player scores a goal, and the entire crowd at Parc des Princes gets to its feet and cheers, was for him the image of absolute happiness. Even just the thought of it sent shivers down his spine.

He would say "stop" or "that's good" instead of "thank you" when I served him at the table. He called me "*la meuf,*" and "*la reum.*"* He was amused by the loud cries I uttered on learning he had smoked hashish. He had never voted and was not on any voters list. He believed that nothing whatsoever about society could be changed, that all he

---

* Verlan: *meuf* means *femme* (woman, wife) and *reum* means *mère* (mother).

had to do was learn its inner workings and play the system—take advantage of the rights it granted to get out of having a job. He was a young man of his times, who lived by the rule of "to each his own shit." Work for him meant nothing more than a constraint with which he did not wish to comply, if other ways of life were possible. Having a profession had been, and remained, the condition of my freedom, given the relative uncertainty of my books meeting with success, though I agreed that student life had seemed to me richer and more pleasurable.

Thirty years earlier I would have turned away from him. Then, I would not have wanted to be confronted with the signs of my working-class origins in a boy—everything that I found "hickish" and knew I'd once had in me too. The fact that he sometimes wiped his mouth with a piece of bread or put his finger over his glass so I wouldn't serve him more wine didn't matter to me at all. That I noticed those signs—and perhaps, more subtly still, was indifferent to them—proved that I no longer inhabited the same world as him. With my husband, I had felt like a working-class girl; with A., I was a *bourge*.

He embodied the memory of my first world. Shaking sugar into his coffee so that it melted more quickly, chopping up his spaghetti, slicing an apple into little pieces and spearing them with the point of his knife, were all gestures I had forgotten and found again in him, disturbingly. I was ten or fifteen years old again, sitting at the table with my family, my cousins whose white skin A. shared, and the red cheeks of the Normans. He incorporated my past.

With him I traveled through all the ages of life, my life.

I took him to the places where I had spent a lot of time in my student years. The Café Métropole and the Donjon, near the train station. The school of literature on rue Beauvoisine, whose building had been decommissioned since the department's transfer to the campus at Mont-Saint-Aignan and, on the outside, remained the same as in the sixties, with its notice board protected by a metal grille, though the clock on the façade had stopped. The little student residence on rue d'Herbouville and, next to it, the university canteen, where, having gone through the entrance and up a few stairs to the front hall, unchanged, with a radiator in the middle and the doors in the same place, for several long minutes I felt myself move through the nameless time of dreams.

Love on the mattress on the floor in the icy bedroom, hasty improvised meals, and childish roughhousing, to which I submitted without difficulty, gave me a sense of repetition. In contrast to the days when I was eighteen, or twenty-five, and completely immersed in anything that happened to me, with neither past nor future, in Rouen, with A., I felt as if I were reenacting scenes and actions already past—from the play of my youth. Or indeed as if I were writing/living a novel whose episodes I was constructing with care. About a weekend at the Grand Hôtel de Cabourg or a trip to Naples. Some of these had already been written, like the one about the getaway to Venice, where I had gone for the first time with a man in 1963, and met a young Italian in 1990. Even taking A. to the Théâtre de la Huchette to see *The Bald Soprano* repeated the ritual I observed with each of my sons when they entered adolescence.

Our relationship could have been considered from the perspective of mutual gain. He gave me pleasure and made me relive things I would never have imagined experiencing again. That I treated him to trips and saved him from looking for a job that would have made him less available to me seemed a fair arrangement, a good deal, especially since it was I who set the rules. I was in a dominant position, and I used the weapons of that dominance, whose fragility, in a romantic relationship, I nonetheless recognized.

I allowed myself to snap at him—I don't know if my harsh retorts had to do with his economic dependence or his youth. "Stop busting my balls!"—a vulgar injunction he was offended by and which I'd never used with anyone before.

I liked to think of myself as *the one* who could change his life.

In more than one domain—literature, theater, bourgeois customs—I was his initiator, but the things I experienced because of him were also initiatory. My main reason for wanting our story to continue was that, in a sense, it was already over and I was a fictional character within it.

I was aware that this entailed a kind of cruelty towards this younger man who was doing things for the first time. Invariably, when he spoke of his plans for a future with me, I replied, "The present is enough," never mentioning that for me the present was only a duplicate of the past. But the duplicity of which he habitually accused me in his fits of jealousy, contrary to what he imagined, did not arise from any desire I may have felt for other men, nor even from memories of past lovers, which he was also convinced I harbored. It was an inherent part of his presence in my life, which he had transformed into a strange and never-ending palimpsest.

When he was at my place, he put on the hooded dressing gown that had enveloped other men. When he wore it, I never saw any of the others in particular. Gazing at the light gray terry cloth, I felt only the sweetness of my own continuity and the consistency of my desire.

Sometimes we talked about the day when he would be married and the father of a child. This future we invoked, looking deep into each other's eyes, holding each other tightly, on the verge of tears, was not at all sad. That we experienced it as something past made the present moment all the more intense and poignant. We communed in our imaginations over our mutual loss with acute pleasure.

My body had become ageless. It took a heavily disapproving look from customers sitting next to us in a restaurant to apprise me of it, a look which far from making me ashamed, reinforced my determination not to hide my affair with a man "who could have been my son," when any fifty-something guy could carry on openly with a woman obviously not his daughter without arousing disapproval. But, looking at this older couple, I knew that if I was with a twenty-five-year-old man, it was so that I would not continually be looking at the timeworn face of a man my age, the face of my own aging. When A.'s face was before me, mine was young too. Men have known this forever, and I saw no reason to deprive myself.

Sometimes, in certain women my age, I perceived the desire to catch his eye. The logic seemed simple enough: "If he likes her, he must prefer mature women, so why not me?" They knew where they stood in the reality of the sexual marketplace, and the fact that one of their sisters had overstepped its boundaries gave them hope and made them bold. As much as I was annoyed by this attitude and the attempts to capture my companion's desire, most of the time discreetly, it disturbed me less than the self-assurance with which young women chatted him up right in front of me, as if the presence of an older woman at his side were a negligible or even nonexistent obstacle. But, when you thought about it, a mature woman appeared to be more dangerous than a young woman, the proof being that he had left one of twenty for me.

We went to see films depicting affairs between young men and older women. We came out disappointed, irritated by story lines in which we found nothing that resembled our experience, films in which the woman begged and pleaded and ended up cast aside, destroyed. Nor was I the Léa of Colette's *Chéri*, which I had reread. What I felt in this relationship was something inexpressible, in which sex, time, and memory were intertwined. Fleetingly, I saw A. as the young man in Pasolini's *Teorema*, a kind of angel of revelation.

Like others who find themselves in situations that contravene the norms of society, we were quick to identify couples similar to us. Conspiratorial glances passed between us. We needed resemblance. When we were in public, it was impossible to forget that we were living out this story of ours before the eyes of society; I took this as a challenge to overturn conventions.

Lying next to him on the beach, I knew our neighbors were watching us covertly, me especially, taking in every detail of my body and assessing its state of advancement, *How old do you reckon she is?* Lying separately on the sand, neither of us would have received more than a passing glance. Faced with the couple we obviously formed, people stared with impudence that verged on stupefaction, as if witnessing a union that defied the order of nature. Or a mystery. What they saw was not us, but, in some tangled way, incest.

One Sunday, in Fécamp, we walked hand in hand down the promenade by the sea, followed from one end to the other by the eyes of people sitting on the low concrete wall that ran the length of the beach. A. remarked that we were more objectionable than a homosexual couple. I remembered another summer Sunday, when I walked between my parents down the same promenade at age eighteen with all eyes upon me because of my very tight dress that had earned me an irritable reproach from my mother for not having worn a girdle which, she said, "covers you up properly." I felt as if I were the same outrageous girl again—this time, without the slightest sense of shame, but a sense of victory.

I was not always so glorious. One afternoon in Capri, before the spectacle of young suntanned women wheeling about the piazzetta where we were drinking Campari, I had snapped: "Tempted by the young ones?" His look of surprise and then his burst of laughter made me realize my mistake. The question was meant to demonstrate my understanding and broad-mindedness and by no means to ascertain where his true desire lay—that, he had proven to me just an hour before. However, not only had it emphasized that I was myself no longer young, but that he too was excluded from the category I had named, as if being with me had removed him from it.

My memory readily supplied me with images of war, American tanks in the Valley, in Lillebonne, posters of General de Gaulle under his képi, the demonstrations of May '68, and I was with someone whose most distant memories, which he struggled to recall, were of the election of Giscard d'Estaing. When I was with A., my memory seemed to me infinite. There was great sweetness to that layer of time which stood between us, it gave more intensity to the present. That my long memory of the time before his birth was, in short, the counterpart, the inverted image of what his own memory would be after my death, with events and political figures I would never know, did not cross my mind. In any case, through his very existence, he *was* my death, as were my sons for me, and as I had been for my mother, who died before having seen the Soviet Union fall but could remember the bells that rang throughout the country on November 11, 1918.

He wanted to have a child with me. This desire troubled me and made me feel the profound unfairness of being in good physical shape but no longer able to conceive. I marveled at the fact that, thanks to science, this could now be accomplished after menopause with another woman's oocyte. But I had no desire to start the procedure my gynecologist had suggested to achieve this end. I simply toyed with the idea of becoming a mother again, something which, after the birth of my second child, at twenty-eight, I had never wanted. As for A., he may have been confusing one desire with another. One summer, in Chioggia, as we were waiting for the vaporetto that would take us back to Venice, he said, "I would like to be inside you and come out of you so I could be like you."

He had shown me photos of himself as a frail child with curls, and as an adolescent scowling through his long hair. I felt no reticence about showing him photos of myself as a little girl and adolescent. For both of us, those were distant times. It took greater effort to bring out photos of myself at twenty, twenty-five, through vanity choosing the prettiest, knowing it was this image that would most cruelly underscore the comparison with my face of the present, harder and more gaunt. It was another girl he saw, whose reality, sought in the woman of today, would always elude him. The desire aroused in him by the girl with the unlined face and long curtain of brown hair, a girl he would never see, that desire was a dead end.

His spontaneous reaction implied as much: "That photo makes me sad."

One day in a brasserie in Madrid where we were having lunch, Nancy Holloway's "Don't Make Me Over" played. I saw the girls' residence in Rouen and myself dazedly searching rue Eau-de-Robec and place Saint-Marc for the shingle of a doctor who would give me an abortion, in November 1963. Kennedy had just been assassinated. I watched A. eating fries across from me. He was not much older than the student lover with whom I'd become pregnant and who, without my knowledge, had etched the Nancy Holloway song, then popular, upon my memory and given it a meaning of mad love and dereliction—the state I was in at the time. I thought that no matter what man I heard it with, the song would never have any other meaning. If, later, on hearing it again, I also remembered the brasserie from Puerta del Sol, with A. sitting across from me, the moment would derive its only value from having been the setting for a violent memory. It would merely be a memory once-removed.

More and more it seemed to me that I could continue to accumulate images, experiences, years, and no longer feel anything but repetition itself. I had the impression of being at once eternal and dead, as my mother is in a dream I often have, and from which I wake up certain, for a few moments, that she really is alive, in this dual form.

This impression was a sign that his role in my life—that of revealing where I stood in

Time—had come to an end. Mine of initiatrix in his life had no doubt ended too. He left
Rouen for Paris.

I started work on the story of the backstreet
abortion that I had hesitated for so long to
write. The further I progressed in writing about
this event that had taken place before A. was
even born, the more strongly—irrepressibly—I
felt that I must leave him, as if wanting to tear
him away from myself and expel him as I'd
done with the embryo, more than thirty years
earlier.

I worked steadily on my story and, through
a resolute strategy of distancing, on ending the
relationship. The breakup coincided, give or
take a few weeks, with the book's completion.

It was autumn, the last of the twentieth century. I found that I was happy to be entering the third millennium alone and free.

1998–2000
2022

BIOGRAPHY

I was born in 1940 in Lillebonne, a small working-class town twenty-five kilometers from Le Havre. I was an only child and my parents, Alphonse and Blanche Duchesne, ran a small café-grocery store in the spinning mill district. They had lost a little girl of seven before I was born. My first memories are inseparable from the war, the bombings that devastated Normandy in 1944.

After the war, my parents returned to Yvetot, which lies between Le Havre and Rouen, the town where they both were born and had worked in a factory. I lived there for my entire childhood, until age eighteen, moving back and forth between two socially opposite milieux, the food and beverage establishment run by my parents, located on the outskirts of town, and the private Catholic boarding school in the city center where they had enrolled me.

with my father, 1949

Very quickly I showed an aptitude for study and a love of reading, encouraged by my mother. Of poor health, I was spoiled with books and nice clothes acquired at the cost of sacrifices on the part of my parents.

with my mother, 1959

At eighteen, after completing the first part of the *baccalauréat*, I left for high school in Rouen to do the second part, in philosophy. So began two years of deep emotional suffering, with bouts of bulimia followed by periods of anorexia. But Simone de Beauvoir's *Second Sex* was a revelation that opened my eyes to "a world made by men and for men."

At nineteen, with no plans or desires, I entered the École normale for schoolteachers in Rouen as a boarder. Unable to bear the close-minded spirit of the place, I left in the middle of the school year. That is how I ended up in Finchley, on the outskirts of London, cleaning house all morning but unoccupied for the rest of the day. I read a great deal of contemporary French literature, of which there was a well-stocked section in the Finchley lending library. At the end of the summer, from that vacuum was born my desire to write a novel, interrupted when I returned to France to enter the literature department at the University of Rouen. I was a scholarship student and for the sake of my parents, felt obliged to pass my exams and get a job.

1962

In October 1962, I resumed work on the novel begun in England. Completed in four months, it was refused by two or three publishers. In June 1963, I obtained a degree in modern literature. The vision I had of my future then was that of a woman who writes while earning her living as a teacher.

The following summer, I met a political science student in Bordeaux, Philippe Ernaux. Pregnant, intent on finishing my studies at a time when abortion was prohibited in France, I resorted to a backstreet abortionist, called in French *une faiseuse d'anges*.

I married Philippe Ernaux in 1964, and our first child, Eric, was born on December 25th of the same year. We were still students, and lived in Bordeaux in difficult material conditions. I failed the *agrégation*;* my husband obtained his degree in political science.

In 1965, we left for Annecy, a tourist town in the Alps, where my husband had landed an administrative position. At the end of June 1967, having been accepted for the competitive exams to qualify as a teacher of literature, I went to Yvetot to see my parents. The next morning, my father had a heart attack and he died three days later. I was aware of this being the most violent and unspeakable separation I would ever know in my life. In September

---

* The highest teaching diploma in France.

with Eric and David, 1968

I was assigned a teaching position in a high school forty kilometers from my home.

In May 1968, my participation in the events that caused such upheaval in France was only from a distance because I was expecting a second child, who would be born in October, David. A year later, I was appointed to a teaching post in Annecy. My mother came to live with us and took on a large part of the childcare. This allowed me to study, once again, for the *agrégation de lettres*, which I obtained in 1971, and, in the spring of 1972, to start writing the book I had constantly thought about in the past four years. I wrote it in secret, on the afternoons when I had no classes, and mailed it to three publishers. It was published as *Les armoires vides* [*Cleaned Out*], by Gallimard, in April 1974. I was thirty-three years old.

In 1975, we moved to a new town, Cergy-Pontoise, still under construction, and during the summer of 1976, I wrote a second book, *Ce qu'ils disent ou rien* [*Do What They Say or Else*]. I had little time to write because of my teaching work, the children and domestic chores. This situation, common among women, of assuming the material burden of family life along with the demands of a profession, inspired the book *La femme gelée* [*A Frozen Woman*], published in 1981.

This book foreshadowed the change I would make in my life, in my early forties. I separated

November 1984

from my husband and lived with my sons. That is when I found a form for the book about my father. Entitled *La place* [*A Man's Place*], it marks a break, which would prove definitive, from the novelistic genre. In spite of its success, I chose to keep my teaching job so I would never have to depend on commercial success.

After that, my books arrived at irregular intervals. *Une femme* [*A Woman's Story*], about my mother, who had Alzheimer's disease and died in 1986; *Passion simple* [*Simple Passion*], *Journal du dehors* [*Exteriors*], *La honte* [*Shame*], *L'evenement* [*Happening*]. They were more numerous starting in 2000 with my retirement from teaching: *L'occupation* [*The Possession*], *L'écriture comme un couteau*, *L'usage de la photo*. I was able to successfully complete the writing of *Les Années* [*The Years*], a collective historical and social autobiography.

Since 1977, I have lived and written in the same house in the heights of Cergy-Pontoise.

WORKS BY ANNIE ERNAUX

In order of publication in English, followed by the dates of original publication in French.

Cleaned Out, 1974

A Woman's Story, 1987

A Man's Place, 1983

Simple Passion, 1991

A Frozen Woman, 1981

Exteriors, 1993

Shame, 1997